THE HEINZ®
TOMATO
KETCHUP
COOKBOOK

PAUL HARTLEY

TEN SPEED PRESS
Berkeley | Toronto

CONTENTS

ACKNOWLEDGMENTS

First to Lynda, my wife, who has patiently shopped, written, washed up, cooked, and recooked all these dishes with me, adding her special touch to make each recipe complete. A huge thanks to Paul Harvey at Heinz, who encouraged me and gave me the privileged opportunity to write this book. Thank you to Andy Jones, a great chum and an excellent chef, who has helped solve all sorts of technical foodie issues. And now thank you to my beloved labrador, Tiffy, who has stood by me for hours on end, waiting for tidbits to fall from my pans, and to all those most precious friends and family who have served on my Heinz Tomato Ketchup tasting panels over many lunches and dinners.

Finally, to the help and encouragement from our publishers at Absolute Press, always there, always ready to guide and advise: thank you, Jon Croft, Meg Avent, and especially Matt Inwood, whose design and care have created such a fantastic book. Also, my grateful appreciation to Sara Golski at Ten Speed Press, who has diligently worked with me to gently adapt this cookbook for an American audience.

All food photography © Peter Cassidy.

Images on pages 36, 42, 47, 59, 70 supplied by The History of Advertising Trust from the Heinz collection held at HAT.

Image on page 45: © 2006 Claudia Elliot, Photograph © 2007 Carnegie Museum of Art, Pittsburgh. Luke Swank, *Still Life: Heinz Ketchup Display*, c. 1930 Carnegie Museum of Art, Pittsburgh, Gift of Edith Swank Long by transfer from the Pennsylvania Department, Carnegie Library of Pittsburgh.

Image on page 67: photography by Kevin Summers.

All other images courtesy of Heinz.

INTRODUCTION

One of the joys of being a food writer is delving into the history of iconic food brands that grace kitchens the world over, and Heinz Tomato Ketchup certainly falls into this category. Created more than 130 years ago, it's still going strong.

It is more than probable that ketchup originated from Asia, probably China, and was called *ke-tsiap*. It was a spicy pickled fish sauce. The early merchant sailors discovered it and brought it to the West, where tomatoes were added, and the ketchup we know today evolved from there.

I've loved seeing red in my studio kitchen as each recipe was created, tried, and enhanced by a good dollop of ketchup.

The result was developing more intense flavors in traditional British dishes like Bangers and Mash, adding color to Schnitzel with Noodles, and bringing balance to Golden Egg Boat Curry. I wonder when Henry James Heinz first tasted his new ketchup in 1876 if he knew it was a eureka moment. For all of us who enjoy this great ingredient it certainly was. Ketchup has brought both flavor and color to the kitchen table ever since.

I have loved writing this book and sharing Heinz Tomato Ketchup–infused dishes with friends around the barbecue or breakfast table, over long summer lunches and dinners in front of a log fire. I hope these recipes inspire you to see how versatile ketchup can be.

THE TOMATO KETCHUP YEARS...

1844 Henry John Heinz is born in a small village outside Pittsburgh, Pennsylvania.

1869 Henry J. Heinz founds the company. The first product is horseradish, presented in clear glass bottles. Competitors chose to conceal the contents of their jars behind green glass. By opting for transparency, the quality of Heinz's product was clear for all to see.

1876 Heinz launches Tomato Ketchup as part of his range. The ketchup was intended as a convenience food, as a "blessed relief for mother and other women in the household," since making ketchup in those days was an arduous and messy affair.

1882 Heinz patents the design of his glass ketchup bottle.

1890 The brand identity comes together with the development of the keystone logo. Also, the screw cap is introduced.

1898 Heinz proudly announces that there is no condiment more universally popular than ketchup.

1905 Heinz is producing more than 5 million bottles worldwide. By 1907, output would more than double.

1919 At the age of 75, and with his food factory one of the largest in America, Henry J. Heinz dies of pneumonia. He is succeeded by his son, Howard.

1925 The company becomes increasingly successful under the control of Howard. Branches begin to open all over the world, including a large purpose-built factory in Harlesden, England, which would go on to survive two bombing attacks during World War II.

1948 With the war over, Heinz begins to produce Tomato Ketchup at a former munitions factory in the northeast English town of Standish.

1957 Heinz celebrates the year 1957 in style. With the "57 Varieties" tag to the fore, Heinz plasters the press with ads for its products, even beginning a TV campaign on New Year's Day.

1972 The company passes the billion-dollar sales mark.

1987 Heinz launches the plastic bottle with flip-top cap, an innovation that will enable its customers to get to their beloved ketchup quicker with one big squeeze!

2003 Heinz launches the top-down bottle for instant application without any mess around the lid.

2006 Heinz Tomato Ketchup is 130 years old! Heinz launches the "Have Your Say" promotion, inviting customers to create witty and creative labels for bottles of ketchup, eight of which, such as "TAKE ME TO YOUR BURGER," make it into print, onto labels, and onto retail shelves.

A LITTLE HEINZ HISTORY

STARTERS

PERFECT SHRIMP COCKTAIL

One of the great starters—shrimp layered with a rich aurora sauce. Aurora is the rosy glow that just precedes the dawn. This is a perfect sauce to serve with shrimp cocktail or a platter of smoked fish.

SERVES 4

AURORA SAUCE
4 tablespoons mayonnaise
3 tablespoons Heinz Tomato Ketchup
1 heaping teaspoon tomato puree
1 level teaspoon prepared horseradish
Generous dash Worcestershire sauce
Salt and freshly ground black pepper
1 teaspoon lemon juice
Zest of $1/2$ lemon
Pinch of smoked paprika

SALAD
Crispy lettuce such as iceberg, romaine,
    or Little Gem
2 ripe medium tomatoes, chopped
1 pound shrimp, cooked and peeled
1 ripe avocado, sliced (only peel it when you
    are ready to use it, as it will quickly discolor)
Parsley and lemon slices, for garnish

To make the aurora sauce, mix all the ingredients together in a bowl and taste, then adjust the seasonings as needed. Leave to stand in a cool place for at least half an hour so that the flavors can meld, but make sure you serve at room temperature.

To assemble the salad, in glasses or glass bowls, put a layer of lettuce, then a layer of chopped tomato, more lettuce, a layer of shrimp, a layer of sliced avocado, then lettuce again, and top with a good layer of shrimp. Drizzle generously with the aurora sauce and finish with a flourish of chopped parsley and a lemon slice. Perfect.

WILD MUSHROOM DIABLO

Mixed wild mushrooms, sautéed in a fiery, creamy sauce.

SERVES 2

1/2 pound mixed fresh wild and
　field mushrooms
2 tablespoons Heinz Tomato Ketchup
1/4 teaspoon soy sauce
1 level teaspoon dry mustard powder
Generous pinch cayenne pepper
2 tablespoons butter
6 tablespoons heavy cream or crème fraîche
2 teaspoons chopped fresh parsley, for garnish
Wedges of warm crusty bread, for dunking

First clean the mushrooms. Do not wash them, just remove any specs of soil with a damp cloth, trim the stems, and break up any larger mushrooms.

In a small bowl, mix together the ketchup, soy sauce, mustard, and cayenne. Heat the butter in a frying pan. When it just begins to foam, add the mushrooms and sauté gently for 5 minutes.

Reduce the heat a little, stir in the ketchup mixture, and cook for 1 minute. Add the cream and continue cooking for a couple of minutes longer. Taste the sauce—you can add more cayenne, if you wish.

Pour the mushrooms into warmed soup bowls and garnish with the parsley. Serve with the bread.

SHAKE. WAIT. SPLOTCH.

Shake, shake the ketchup bottle / First none'll come, and then a lot'll. This charming little couplet was the work of U.S. humorist Richard Willard Armour. It was inspired, however, by fellow countryman and humorist Ogden Nash, who had, some years earlier and rather more succinctly, written: *The Catsup Bottle / First a little / Then a lottle.* Of course, today, Nash and Armour would have had the choice of shaking and waiting or squeezing for instant ketchup gratification.

PORK AND APPLE MEATLOAF

What a great combination! Serve this as a hot starter or a cold lunch.

SERVES 6 TO 8

1 onion, grated
1 tablespoon olive oil
1 pound ground pork
$1/2$ pound cooked white rice
  (about 2 ounces uncooked)
2 green apples, peeled, cored, and grated
2 medium eggs, beaten
2 tablespoons Heinz Tomato Ketchup
Generous dash of Worcestershire sauce
Generous pinch freshly grated nutmeg
1 heaping teaspoon dried Italian herbs
Salt and plenty of freshly ground black pepper

Preheat the oven to 375°F. In a skillet, fry the onion in the olive oil for 3 to 4 minutes until soft. In a large bowl, combine all the remaining ingredients, add the onion, and thoroughly mix together with your hands or a wooden spoon.

Butter a 1-pound loaf pan, press the mixture into it, and bake in the center of the oven, uncovered, for $1^{1}/_{4}$ hours. Remove from the oven, allow to cool slightly, and then remove from the pan. You can serve this warm or cold with a mixed salad. It makes a great starter or a lovely lunch, and it's perfect fried in slices for breakfast. It will keep for 4 to 5 days in the fridge.

BEST BUDDIES #1

THE BURGER. Ground meat was eaten in the days of the Egyptian pharoahs. Meat patties can be traced back to the Mongol empire, and placing them between bread allowed armies to eat while they marched. Fast-forward to the eighteenth century, to the German town of Hamburg, which gave the snack its name: patties were made of ground beef, onion, and bread crumbs. Emigrants took the burger to America; its convenience as a quick handheld snack took off, and ketchup finally crowned its glory!

| 1870- | 1883- | 1888- | 1889- |
| 1876 | 1905 | 1895 | 1910 |

1914-
1920

1944 to
Present

1983 to
Present

1985 to
Present

SOUPS
AND
SALADS

GAZPACHO WITH ANCHOVY CROUTONS

A chilled explosion of fresh vegetable flavor with salty croutons.

SERVES 6

2 pounds vine-ripened tomatoes
2 cloves garlic, crushed
1 cup fresh white bread crumbs
2 tablespoons red wine vinegar
3 tablespoons extra-virgin olive oil
1/2 cucumber, peeled, seeded, and chopped
2 green onions, thinly sliced
1 red bell pepper, finely chopped
1 yellow bell pepper, finely chopped
1 tablespoon chopped fresh flat-leaf parsley
1 tablespoon torn basil leaves
1 cup ice water
2 tablespoons Heinz Tomato Ketchup
1/2 teaspoon celery salt
Freshly ground black pepper

CROUTONS
10 anchovy fillets
2 tablespoons butter
4 thick slices stale bread, crusts removed
Olive oil, to spread on baking sheet

Handful of ice cubes

Peel and seed the tomatoes—the easy way is to pour boiling water over them in a bowl and leave for a minute until the skins can be peeled away from the flesh. Put all the ingredients, except the celery salt and black pepper, into a blender and whirl until pureed. Now add the celery salt and pepper to taste. (Bear in mind that you are going to be adding anchovy croutons, which are salty.) Pour the soup into a large bowl, cover, and chill.

To make the croutons, preheat the oven to 400°F. Lay the anchovies in a small frying pan and sauté with the butter—you will find that they almost dissolve. Spread the anchovy butter all over the bread and cut into 1/2-inch cubes. Scatter the cubes on an oiled baking sheet and bake in the oven for about 5 minutes, then flip them over. Keep an eye on them, as they will turn color very suddenly. Allow to cool.

To serve, pour the chilled gazpacho into soup bowls, add a couple of ice cubes to each dish, and then scatter the croutons over the gazpacho.

it's RED MAGIC time!

Heinz Ketchup ...made fresh from sun-ripened tomatoes

Stock up now on these famous Red Magic Values!

WE'VE JUST HARVESTED a bumper crop of big, beautiful red-ripe tomatoes, specially grown from Heinz own pedigreed seeds.

• These pampered sun-ripened tomatoes have been made into richer, thicker Heinz Ketchup, extra-spicy

Heinz *Hot* Ketchup and zesty Heinz Chili Sauce.

• **Now** it's your turn to harvest the values your food store has on these famous *red magic* condiments.

No other Ketchup tastes like Heinz!

It's only natural...

You won't find anything artificial about Heinz Tomato Ketchup. No artificial thickeners. No artificial preservatives. No artificial colouring. No artificial flavour. They just don't grow in Heinz ketchup bottles.

It's only good natural ingredients you'll find there. A few homely spices and a whole lot of tomatoes. In fact, we use a pound and a half of good ripe tomatoes to make just three-quarters of a pound of thick, rich Heinz ketchup.

You can't improve on nature, we reckon.

No other ketchup tastes like Heinz

COCONUT, CHILE, AND SQUASH SOUP

A thick, spicy, and filling soup with flavors that will dance on your taste buds.

SERVES 4 TO 6

2 tablespoons vegetable oil
2 shallots, sliced
2 green onions, sliced
2 cloves garlic, peeled and crushed (optional)
$^3/_4$-inch piece fresh ginger, peeled
   and finely diced
1 Thai chile, seeded and finely diced
1 pound butternut squash, peeled, seeded,
   and cut into $^3/_4$-inch cubes
1 cup vegetable broth
1 tablespoon Thai fish sauce
3 tablespoons Heinz Tomato Ketchup
$1^3/_4$ cups unsweetened coconut milk
Handful of fresh cilantro
Zest and juice of 1 lime

Heat the oil in a large saucepan and add the shallots, onions, garlic, ginger, and chile. Cook gently for 5 to 6 minutes until soft, and then toss in the butternut squash and stir around for a couple of minutes.

Add the broth, fish sauce, ketchup, and coconut milk and simmer, covered, for 30 minutes. Roughly chop the cilantro, reserving a little for garnish, and add it to the soup together with the lime zest and juice.

Remove from the heat and allow the mixture to cool enough to puree into a smooth soup. Reheat when ready to serve and garnish with the remaining cilantro.

MARILYN, ELVIS, AND HEINZ

In the mid-1960s, Andy Warhol started on a series of sculptures that transformed ordinary objects into art. He employed carpenters to construct plywood boxes onto which he painted the logos of different consumer products, making them identical to supermarket cartons. When Heinz Tomato Ketchup was immortalized in such a way, it took its place in the Pop Art Pantheon alongside Warhol's other twentieth-century icons such as Elvis Presley and Marilyn Monroe.

PASTRAMI, ARUGULA, AND RED CHARD SALAD WITH RYE CROUTONS

Sumptuous starter with big flavor and a thick herb and tomato dressing.

SERVES 4

TOMATO AND GINGER VINAIGRETTE

1 large vine-ripened tomato, peeled and
    seeded (see page 10)
1 teaspoon grated fresh ginger
2 tablespoons Heinz Tomato Ketchup
1 tablespoon balsamic vinegar
2 teaspoons red wine vinegar
Freshly ground black pepper
2 tablespoons olive oil
Salt

CROUTONS

2 slices rye bread
Sea salt
Olive oil

SALAD

2 handfuls of arugula leaves
1 handful of red chard leaves
1 handful of baby lettuce leaves
1 red onion, sliced into slivers
$2/3$ pound pastrami, thinly sliced

To make the vinaigrette, place all the ingredients in a blender except the olive oil and the salt. Blend together, adding the olive oil in a steady stream, until you have a thick sauce. Now add a pinch or two of salt and taste (if you add the salt earlier it may stop the mixture from emulsifying). This vinaigrette will keep for several days in the fridge, but be sure to bring it back to room temperature before serving.

To prepare the croutons, preheat the oven to 400°F. Remove the crusts and then cut the rye bread into cubes of about $1/2$ inch. Spread them on a baking sheet, sprinkle with a generous pinch of sea salt, and drizzle with olive oil. Bake for about 10 minutes, until golden. Drain on paper towels.

Mix the salad leaves and onion together in a large bowl, spoon over the dressing, and toss. Divide the salad among 4 plates, arrange strips of pastrami over the top, and scatter with the rye croutons.

We know exactly where it came from.

It knows exactly where it's going.

We don't have to play ketchup.

ROASTED RED PEPPER SALAD

A stylish Provençal salad finished with a flourish of roasted red peppers.

SERVES 4 TO 6

$^3/_4$ cup Madeira wine
$^1/_3$ cup red wine vinegar
1 tablespoon Heinz Tomato Ketchup
2 teaspoons Demerara sugar
1 ($2^1/_2$-inch) cinnamon stick
2 whole cloves
Generous pinch grated nutmeg
$^1/_3$ cup light olive oil
3 to 4 red bell peppers
Mixed lettuce leaves
2 ounces hard goat cheese
2 ounces shelled walnuts, lightly crushed

Pour into a small saucepan the Madeira, vinegar, ketchup, sugar, and spices and bring to a boil, stirring to dissolve the sugar. Keep boiling until the liquid is reduced by half, to about $^2/_3$ cup. Leave to cool.

Remove and discard the cinnamon stick and cloves and transfer the remaining liquid to a blender. Gradually add the olive oil while the blender is running. You can make this vinaigrette the day before and keep in the fridge, but you must bring it back to room temperature before using or you will lose some of the flavor.

Roast the red peppers until just blackened all over. You can use tongs over a gas flame, a hot grill, or a dry griddle pan—whichever suits you. Carefully transfer the peppers to a bowl, cover with plastic wrap, and leave for 10 minutes. After this time, you will find you can remove the skin easily with a sharp knife, working down from the stem, which can be discarded together with any seeds and pith from inside the pepper. Cut the peppers into strips, put into a bowl, and pour the vinaigrette over them. Leave for half an hour to infuse the flavors.

Arrange the salad leaves on plates, and lift the peppers from the dressing and lay them on top. Using a potato peeler, shave off thin strips of goat cheese and scatter them over the salad together with the walnuts. Drizzle the vinaigrette over and around the salad and serve.

Serve the salad as a fun lunch with some soft, warm focaccia bread or a deliciously light starter for dinner.

AT THE 1893 CHICAGO WORLD'S FAIR, MORE THAN 1,000,000 HEINZ PICKLE PINS WERE HANDED OUT: A PROMOTIONAL PHENOMENON!

BRUNCH
AND
LUNCH

BREAKFAST TOMATO AND POTATO WAFFLES

Easy-to-make savory potato waffles.

SERVES 6

1/4 pound all-purpose flour
1 rounded teaspoon baking powder
Pinch salt
1 egg
1/3 cup milk mixed with 3 tablespoons
   Heinz Tomato Ketchup
1 tablespoon vegetable oil
1/3 pound cooked mashed potato
Freshly ground black pepper

The waffles can be prepared in advance and frozen. Simply defrost and heat before serving.

To make the waffle batter, in a bowl mix together the flour, baking powder, and salt. Next add the egg and then the milk and ketchup mixture a little at a time, and beat until you have a smooth batter. Now add the oil and the potato, and season with pepper. Mix well (your batter will no longer be smooth). Chill in the fridge for at least 2 hours or overnight, until ready for breakfast.

Heat a lightly oiled waffle iron until it just begins to smoke a little (or heat an electric waffle maker as instructed), then spoon in about 1/3 cup batter mixture and close the lid. It will spread out on its own to a lovely oval shape. If you want a perfect rectangular waffle, it's better to spread the mixture yourself to cover the complete base of the waffle iron. Cook each side over medium-high heat for 3 minutes, turning only once, so that they are golden brown and cooked through. Repeat until the mixture is used up, keeping the waffles warm.

These waffles are delicious topped with grilled mushrooms, some cherry tomatoes, or a pile of scrambled eggs.

THE WORLD'S LARGEST KETCHUP BOTTLE: COLLINSVILLE, ILLINOIS, BUILT IN 1949 ON TOP OF A WATER TOWER AND STANDING 170 FEET TALL

TOMATO KETCHUP. (IMPERIAL STYLE.)

HUEVOS FLAMENCA

If you love brunch, then you will love this Spanish-influenced dish to share. Big on taste, big on the eyes, and big on the table.

SERVES 4

1 tablespoon olive oil
1 large onion, roughly chopped
1 red bell pepper, cut into $3/4$-inch-
   square chunks
1 green bell pepper, cut into $3/4$-inch-
   square chunks
1 hot chile pepper, seeded and finely diced
Salt and freshly ground black pepper
$1/3$ pound smoked bacon, cut into
   $3/4$-inch strips
2 large tomatoes, diced
3 tablespoons Heinz Tomato Ketchup
Dash of Worcestershire sauce
1 tablespoon torn basil leaves
4 eggs
Crusty bread, for serving

In a large, heavy frying pan, heat the oil over medium heat and fry the onion, bell peppers, and chile pepper for about 15 minutes until softened, stirring occasionally. Season to taste with salt and pepper.

While this is cooking, fry the bacon in a separate pan until crispy and golden, then remove, drain on paper towels, and keep warm.

Now return to the original pan and add in the tomatoes, ketchup, Worcestershire sauce, and basil leaves. Stir well and cook for 5 minutes longer—do not let it burn, but give it a chance for all the wonderful flavors to fuse together.

Here's the clever bit! Press a ladle firmly into the mixture in order to make 4 nests. Now crack one egg at a time into the bowl of the ladle and carefully turn the ladle into the nest to settle the egg. Repeat with the other eggs and cover immediately, cooking for 3 to 4 minutes longer to poach the eggs until the whites have set and the yolks are still runny.

Serve this stunning brunch or lunch dish by putting the pan in the center of the table for everybody to dig into with slices of crusty warm bread.

CHORIZO AND SUMMER VEGETABLE OMELET

A regional Spanish omelet served hot or cold—a summer spectacular.

SERVES 4 TO 6

3 tablespoons olive oil
1 Spanish onion, sliced
Salt and freshly ground black pepper
1 pound waxy potatoes, peeled,
    cut into $1/4$-inch slices, rinsed,
    and dried
6 large eggs
Handful of fava beans, blanched
Handful of frozen peas, defrosted
4 teaspoons Heinz Tomato Ketchup
2 tomatoes, sliced
2 ounces chorizo, thinly sliced

Heat 1 tablespoon of the oil in a large deep nonstick frying pan; add the onion and fry gently for 6 to 8 minutes until soft and golden. Season well with salt and pepper. Transfer the onion to a bowl.

Using the same pan, add the remaining 2 tablespoons olive oil and sauté half the potatoes at a time until golden. Drain the potatoes on paper towels and then add them to the onion.

In a separate bowl, whisk the eggs and season well. Now add the eggs, beans, and peas to the potatoes and onion and carefully mix together.

Preheat the broiler. Reheat the large frying pan and then pour in the omelet mixture. Decrease the heat and cook the omelet for 4 to 6 minutes, until the base is set and the egg on top is still runny. Remove the pan from the heat, spoon on 4 big blobs of ketchup, and marble in with a fork. Lay the tomatoes and chorizo on top. Put under the broiler for 4 to 6 minutes, until the top sets and just starts to turn golden. Cut into wedges and serve hot or cold for the perfect summer lunch.

HEINZ TOMATO KETCHUP HAS A SPEED LIMIT: IF IT POURS UNAIDED AT MORE THAN .028 MPH, IT'S REJECTED!

LAMB AND MINT BRUNCH BURGERS WITH RIVERSIDE SALSA

Perfect homemade burgers teased with fresh mint.

SERVES 4

RIVERSIDE SALSA

1 medium onion, finely diced
$1/3$ cucumber, peeled and finely diced
$1/2$ green apple, peeled, cored, and
    finely diced
2 teaspoons lime juice
2 teaspoons mango chutney, large lumps cut up
1 tablespoon chopped fresh cilantro leaves
$1/2$ teaspoon roasted cumin seeds
1 teaspoon sweet tamarind sauce
2 tablespoons Heinz Tomato Ketchup

BURGERS

$1 1/2$ pounds ground lamb
1 large onion, grated
1 heaping teaspoon Dijon mustard
1 heaping teaspoon good-quality mint sauce
$1/4$ teaspoon celery salt
Freshly ground black pepper
$1/2$ teaspoon anchovy paste
2 tablespoons Heinz Tomato Ketchup
Dash of Worcestershire sauce
1 large egg, lightly beaten
1 tablespoon all-purpose flour
Vegetable oil, for frying

4 sesame seed buns, warmed

For the salsa, in a bowl mix the onion, cucumber, and apple, add the lime juice (to stop the apple from browning), and toss together. In a separate bowl, mix together the remaining salsa ingredients, then combine everything together, and you are ready to go. This is a really fresh-tasting salsa, but it will only last a day in the fridge.

For the burgers, in a large bowl, break up the lamb, then add the onion, mustard, mint sauce, celery salt, pepper, anchovy paste, ketchup, and Worcestershire sauce and mix together well using your hands or a wooden spoon. Now add the egg and sprinkle the flour evenly, mixing all the ingredients together well. Divide the mixture into 4 equal portions and, using your hands, mold into patties about $1/2$ inch thick. Place on waxed paper and refrigerate for 1 hour or until you are ready to cook them.

Heat a griddle or heavy frying pan with a little oil and when hot cook the burgers over medium to high heat. This should take no longer than 8 minutes, turning once. As it is lamb, don't overcook it—the burgers are better if still a little pink in the middle but golden on the outside. Remove and serve on warmed sesame seed buns topped with the salsa.

SEAFOOD

TUNA CROQUETTES

Tuna with parsley, potatoes, and tomato ketchup, in a crispy crust.

SERVES 6 (MAKES 12 CROQUETTES)

1¼ pound potatoes, peeled and
cut into chunks
1 egg
2 tablespoons unsalted butter, at
room temperature
1 pound fresh tuna steaks, about ¾ inch thick
1 teaspoon anchovy paste
2 tablespoons Heinz Tomato Ketchup
2 tablespoons chopped fresh parsley
Freshly ground black pepper
Seasoned flour, for coating
2 eggs, beaten
Fresh white bread crumbs
Vegetable oil, for frying

Cook the potatoes in boiling salted water for 15 to 20 minutes, until tender. Drain, return them to the pot, and mash together with the egg and butter.

In the meantime, preheat the broiler. Broil the tuna steaks for 3 to 4 minutes on each side until just cooked through. Leave to cool. Break into small flakes.

In a large bowl, spread out the mashed potatoes, adding the tuna flakes. In a small bowl, mix together the anchovy paste, ketchup, and parsley and dollop it onto the tuna mixture. Season with plenty of pepper. Fold all the ingredients together well—a rubber spatula is perfect for this.

Using wet hands to stop the mixture from sticking to you, mold into croquettes, a bit like thick homemade hamburgers, approximately ¼ pound each. Dip the croquettes into the seasoned flour, then into the beaten eggs, and finally into the bread crumbs, making sure they are evenly coated. Chill in the fridge for 30 minutes to set the bread crumbs.

You can either shallow-fry or deep-fry the croquettes in the oil when ready. Cook in batches for 4 to 5 minutes, until the coating is golden and crispy. Drain on paper towels. Great served with a leafy green salad, wedges of lemon, good tartar sauce, or sweet chile dipping sauce.

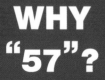

WHY "57"?

THE STORY GOES THAT **Henry Heinz was riding a New York elevated train one day when he noticed an advertisement for a shoe company boasting a variety of 21 styles. He considered this and started to count all the products that the Heinz company was producing. He concluded that there were about 57 (there were actually far more, but the numbers "5" and "7" had a lucky charm for him!). Hence, the birth of the slogan "57 VARIETIES."**

CLAM AND TOMATO GNOCCHI

Baby clams, vine-ripened tomatoes, and potato pasta, all in a luscious cream sauce.

SERVES 2 TO 3

1 pound fresh clams
2 vine-ripened tomatoes, peeled and
    seeded (see page 10)
1 pound fresh gnocchi
3 ounces frozen petite peas
$3/4$ cup heavy cream
1 tablespoon Heinz Tomato Ketchup
1 tablespoon freshly grated Parmesan cheese
Salt and freshly ground black pepper
Sprigs of fresh dill

First prepare the clams by washing them thoroughly in cold water, discarding any broken or open ones. Put the clams into a large pan over medium heat, add a splash of water, and cover. Over a 6-to 8-minute period, shake the pan once or twice until all the clams are fully open. Remove them with a slotted spoon, discarding any that have failed to open and leaving the milky liquid in the pan to add to the sauce later. Remove all the meat from the shells, leaving a few per person in their shells for garnish.

Chop the tomatoes, keeping any juice you can.

Bring 2 pans of lightly salted water to a boil, one large and one small. Add the gnocchi to the larger pan and the peas to the smaller one and cook them both for 3 to 4 minutes. Pour the cream into another small pan, add the ketchup, 2 tablespoons of the reserved clam juice, the Parmesan, and the tomatoes and their juice, and warm gently for a few minutes. Taste and season with salt and pepper. Add the shelled clams at the last minute just to warm through.

Drain the gnocchi and peas in a colander and divide among warmed plates. Pour the creamy tomato sauce over the top, arrange the shell-on clams, and scatter over some tiny sprigs of dill before serving.

Among the first of the "57 VARIETIES" products to be introduced by Heinz:

1869 **Horseradish**	1870 **Chow chow pickles**	1870 **Sauerkraut in crocks**
1870 **Sour gherkins**	1870 **Sour onions**	1873 **Vinegar**
1870 **Mixed sour pickles**	1870 **Prepared mustard**	1876 **Tomato ketchup**

MOROCCAN FISH TAGINE

Flavors of the kasbah—with black olives, preserved lemons, and snapper.

SERVES 4

1 tablespoon olive oil, plus extra for brushing
1 medium onion, chopped
4 plum tomatoes, sliced
2 tablespoons Heinz Tomato Ketchup
1 teaspoon ground cumin
1 teaspoon sweet paprika
2 cups fish broth (you could use chicken
    or vegetable)
4 red snapper fillets (about 6 ounces each),
    halved diagonally (mullet or sea bass
    are equally good)
Salt and freshly ground black pepper
12 black olives, pitted and halved
1 tablespoon tahini (sesame paste)
1/2 preserved lemon, finely chopped
1 tablespoon chopped fresh flat-leaf parsley
1 tablespoon chopped fresh cilantro
1 teaspoon chopped fresh mint

Heat the 1 tablespoon of oil in a large pan and fry the onion gently for 5 minutes. Add the tomatoes and cook for a few more minutes. Stir in the ketchup, cumin, and paprika, and then gradually add the broth. Turn the heat up to high for 2 minutes, and then take the pan off the heat and keep warm.

Preheat the broiler, brush the fillets with olive oil, and season with salt and pepper. Broil skin side up for about 5 minutes. While the fish is cooking, add the olives, tahini, preserved lemon, and herbs (reserving just a little of the herbs for garnish) to the sauce in the pan, stir gently, and reheat. Check the seasoning.

Put the fish into four warmed soup bowls, spoon over the sauce, and scatter the remaining herbs over the top. You could also serve this over steamed couscous or bulgur wheat.

CREOLE-STYLE SHRIMP AND SALMON

Big chunks of salmon and tender fresh shrimp cooked in the inspired full-flavored Creole style. A perfect dish for summer evening al fresco dining.

SERVES 4

2 tablespoons vegetable oil
1 medium onion, diced
2 stalks celery, diced
4 green onions, green and white parts sliced
1 green bell pepper, diced
1 clove garlic, finely chopped
4 tomatoes, roughly chopped
3 tablespoons Heinz Tomato Ketchup
1 tablespoon tomato puree
$1^1/_4$ cups fish broth
2 bay leaves
$^1/_2$ teaspoon cayenne pepper
1 tablespoon freshly squeezed lemon juice
Generous dash of Worcestershire sauce
$^1/_4$ teaspoon Tabasco sauce
Salt
$^2/_3$ pound fresh salmon fillets, skinned
   and cut into cubes
$^2/_3$ pound medium-size fresh shrimp,
   peeled and deveined
Hot cooked rice, for serving
Chopped parsley, for garnish

Heat the oil in a heavy pan, add the onion, celery, green onions, bell pepper, and garlic and sauté gently for 10 minutes.

Stir in the tomatoes, ketchup, tomato puree, and broth, and then add the bay leaves, cayenne, lemon juice, Worcestershire sauce, and Tabasco sauce. Bring to a boil, then decrease the heat to low and simmer gently for 45 minutes, stirring occasionally. To create an authentic Creole-style dish, the sauce needs to be thick and rich by simmering and reducing—so cook a little longer if needed. Taste the sauce and season with salt as needed.

Add the salmon cubes and cook for 3 minutes, then add the shrimp and cook for 5 minutes longer, until the shrimp have turned pink and the salmon is tenderly cooked through. Remove the bay leaves and serve on a bed of hot rice, scattered with chopped parsley.

YOU CAN'T EAT WITHOUT IT.

FRAGRANT VERMOUTH MUSSELS

Delicious mussels, poached in vermouth with a fresh and aromatic twist.

SERVES 2 AS A STARTER

³/₄ pound fresh mussels
1 tablespoon olive oil
2 large shallots, finely chopped
1 stalk lemongrass, finely sliced
2 tablespoons Heinz Tomato Ketchup
³/₄ cup dry vermouth
1 tablespoon finely chopped fresh cilantro
    (leaves and stems)
1 tablespoon finely chopped flat-leaf
    parsley
1 lemon (half for zest and half
    for serving wedges)
Crusty bread, for serving

Put the mussels into the sink and cover with fresh cold water. Discard any mussels that are open or damaged or do not close when tapped. Scrape or scrub them clean of any barnacles and pull away any beards, then put the mussels back into clean fresh water.

Heat a saucepan, large enough to hold the mussels, over low heat and add the oil, shallots, and lemongrass. Fry gently until just softened. Add the ketchup, vermouth, cilantro, parsley (reserving a little for garnish), and lemon zest. Increase the heat, and when the liquid is bubbling, add the mussels to the pan. Stir them well in the sauce, then cover and cook over high heat for 6 to 8 minutes, shaking the pan quite vigorously once or twice with the lid on.

As soon as the mussels have opened (discard any that fail to open), transfer them to warm serving bowls with a slotted spoon, pour the sauce all over, and scatter with the remaining parsley. Serve with the lemon wedges and lots of crusty bread for dunking in the sauce.

GRILLED HALIBUT WITH TOMATO AND DILL BUTTER

Chunky halibut, seared and served with provocative dill and tomato aromas.

SERVES 2

1/4 cup (1/2 stick) unsalted butter,
   at room temperature
1 tablespoon Heinz Tomato Ketchup
1 teaspoon chopped fresh dill
2 halibut fillets (about 1/2 pound each)
Olive oil, for brushing
Sea salt
Sprigs of dill, for garnish

Mash together the butter, ketchup, and dill and chill in the fridge for 10 minutes. Remove, scoop out onto plastic wrap, and roll into a fat sausage about 2 1/2 inches long by 1 inch in diameter. Seal it and freeze for 1 hour.

Brush the fish fillets with olive oil and season with salt. Cook them on a hot grill pan, skin side up, for 2 minutes, turn, and repeat for 3 to 4 minutes more, depending on the thickness of the fillets. Remove the pan from the heat, leaving the fillets in the pan for 1 minute more.

Take the tomato butter from the freezer, leave to stand for a couple of minutes, and slice off rounds less than 1/2 inch thick. Place the halibut fillets on warm serving plates and lay 3 slices of tomato butter on each fillet, topped with a sprig of dill. This is a delicious dish to serve with some crunchy stir-fry vegetables such as snow peas, baby corn, bean sprouts, or broccoli.

ATTACK OF THE KILLER TOMATOES WAS A 1978 FILM THAT SPAWNED THREE SEQUELS!

POULTRY

SPICY GINGER AND ORANGE CHICKEN

Just a delicious chicken casserole with heavenly exotic flavors.

SERVES 6

6 skinless, bone-in chicken breasts
   (allow about $1/2$ pound per person)
1 tablespoon light corn syrup
2 tablespoons Heinz Tomato Ketchup
1 teaspoon ground allspice
1 teaspoon ground cinnamon
$3/4$ cup freshly squeezed orange juice
   (about 2 medium juicy oranges)
1 heaping teaspoon finely grated fresh ginger
Sea salt and freshly ground black pepper

Preheat the oven to 350°F. Put the chicken into a large ovenproof dish.

Mix together the syrup, ketchup, allspice, and cinnamon to make a paste. Gradually stir in the orange juice and then add the ginger, mix well, season to taste with salt and pepper, and spoon over the chicken.

Cover the dish with foil and cook for 30 minutes, basting the chicken with the juices a few times. Then remove the foil and cook for 10 minutes longer.

Lift out the chicken and keep warm. Pour the remaining juices into a saucepan and boil rapidly to reduce by half, making them into a thick, spoonable sauce. Serve the chicken doused in the ginger and orange sauce. This is scrumptious with roasted sweet potato wedges and a simple endive salad.

ART IN THE BEST POSSIBLE TASTE

If you're all out of acrylic or oil paints, then look no further than the kitchen cupboard for the tools to rustle up your next masterpiece. That's what artist Jason Baalman decided to do. He found fame after he uploaded a series of time-lapse videos to Internet site YouTube that showed the creation of one of his ketchup-and-fries

STICKY CHICKEN KEBABS

Chunks of chicken with honey, mustard, and tomato ketchup—sticky!

SERVES 4

2 tablespoons runny honey
2 tablespoons Heinz Tomato Ketchup
1 tablespoon Worcestershire sauce
1 heaping teaspoon Dijon mustard
1 tablespoon cider vinegar
$1/4$ teaspoon Tabasco sauce or to taste
Pinch salt and a good grind of
    freshly ground black pepper
4 skinless, bone-in chicken breasts
Hot cooked rice, for serving
Chopped parsley, for garnish

8 bamboo skewers presoaked in water
    to stop them from blackening during
    cooking

In a large shallow dish mix together the honey, ketchup, Worcestershire sauce, mustard, vinegar, and Tabasco and then season with salt and pepper.

Cut the chicken breasts into cubes of approximately 1 inch, then add them to the bowl with the marinade mixture and keep turning them with a spoon until all the chicken is well coated. Cover with plastic wrap and leave to marinate for 1 hour. (You can alternatively leave in the fridge overnight.)

You can either fire up the barbecue or preheat a griddle or skillet.

Thread all the chicken pieces equally onto the skewers, keeping as much of the delicious marinade on them as possible. Cook for 5 to 6 minutes, turning on all sides as you go. Check that the chicken is thoroughly cooked before serving 2 kebabs arranged like crossed swords on a bed of parsley-flecked white rice.

portraits. Hundreds and thousands tuned in to watch Baalman's four minutes of wacky talent. His fast-growing celebrity landed him a spot on *The Late Show* with David Letterman, where he repeated the feat, painting the stage manager while live on air, using ketchup for paint and french fries for paintbrushes. Baalman's other commissions have included working with yeast extract on toast for an Australian client, while another of his YouTube videos shows him painting with just chocolate and a spoon. Baalman has no formal art training. He's also wary of becoming pigeonholed as "that guy who paints with food." If his number of website views and media moments continue to increase, though, it will be a tag that's hard to change.

YOU  and HEINZ 57

together put 2¼lb of tomatoes on the table
to enjoy at every meal!

IT TAKES 2¼ lb. OF TOMATOES to make one 12-oz. bottle of Heinz Tomato Ketchup. Not just ordinary tomatoes, either! They've got to have a full-bodied flavour, a rich, red colour, plenty of juice and almost no seeds.

The tomatoes Heinz use are grown specially for them in Italy and ripened naturally in the warm Mediterranean sunshine. And, apart from a little sugar, matured vinegar and spices, nothing but the pure, whole goodness of 2¼ lb. of tomatoes goes into Heinz Tomato Ketchup. 1/4 or 2/-.

P.S. Don't forget there's Heinz Tomato Chutney too

It's delicious 2/3 or 3/- a bottle

RED THAI DUCK CURRY

Hot and spicy duck with tongue-tingling, fresh Thai flavors.

SERVES 4

1 whole duck, roasted on a rack for
    1¹/₂ hours at 350°F
1³/₄ cups unsweetened coconut milk
1 rounded tablespoon red Thai curry paste
2 red chiles, seeded and sliced
2 tablespoons Heinz Tomato Ketchup
12 cherry tomatoes, halved
Small handful of torn basil leaves
2 kaffir lime leaves, chopped
1 teaspoon brown sugar
2 teaspoons Thai fish sauce
Noodles or rice, for serving

Remove all the meat with the skin from the duck carcass and cut into ¹/₂-inch slices.

Heat half of the coconut milk in a wok or saucepan, add the red curry paste and chiles, and allow to bubble for 2 to 3 minutes over medium heat. Now add the rest of the coconut milk and the ketchup, bring to a boil, and then simmer for 5 minutes.

Add to the wok the duck and the halved tomatoes, return to a boil, then reduce to a simmer, adding the basil, lime leaves, sugar, and fish sauce. Cook for 8 to 10 minutes longer and serve with fluffy rice or noodles.

PAINTING THE TOWN RED

In the nineteenth-century days of vaudeville variety theaters, rotten tomatoes were the clichéd missile of choice, pelting those stage performers deemed to be particularly bad. Into the twentieth century, tomato hurling was being carried out on a far larger scale in the small Spanish town of Buñol—the scene of the world's biggest food fight. La Tomatina is acted out each August in honor of Buñol's patron saint. It's a two-hour, 137-ton tomato-throwing fest that thousands of tourists flock to.

CHICKEN AND MANGO BBQ PIZZA

Taking the traditional pizza to new heights—big and colorful with great contrasting flavors of sweet mango, smoked cheese, and BBQ-marinated chicken—almost too good to eat.

SERVES 4

1 cooked chicken breast (about 1/2 pound)
   (or the equivalent leftover chicken)
2 heaping tablespoons Heinz
   Hot & Spicy BBQ Sauce
1 fresh ripe mango
1 medium red onion
2 ounces mushrooms
1/4 pound mozzarella cheese
2 ounces smoked cheddar cheese
1 (12-inch) uncooked pizza crust
2-3 tablespoons Heinz Tomato Ketchup
Freshly ground black pepper
Fresh oregano, for garnish

One key to easy pizza making is to prepare all the ingredients in bowls so you will be ready to assemble the pizza—so here goes.

Thinly slice the chicken breast, lay the slices in a dish, and cover with the BBQ sauce. Mix together well and leave for at least half an hour to marinate.

While that's happening, preheat the oven to 350°F. Peel and pit the mango and cut the flesh into 1/2-inch cubes—you will need about 2/3 cup for this pizza. Peel and thinly slice the red onion into half-moons, wipe the mushrooms and slice them, and grate the cheeses separately.

Spread the pizza crust generously with ketchup and season with pepper. Sprinkle the grated cheddar evenly over the ketchup and then lay the onions and mushrooms alternately around the pizza base, working toward the center. Next arrange the marinated BBQ chicken over it all and scatter with the cubed mango. Finally, top with the grated mozzarella and pop the pizza into the oven for 10 to 12 minutes, until the cheese bubbles and the crust turns golden brown.

Finish with a flourish of freshly chopped oregano, cut the pizza into wedges, and serve.

TURKEY MEATBALLS WITH TOMATO SAUCE

Minced turkey breast enhanced with a hot fresh tomato sauce.

SERVES 4 TO 6

MEATBALLS
1 pound ground turkey meat
1 onion, grated
1 egg, beaten
2 cups bread crumbs
3 tablespoons Heinz Tomato Ketchup
1 tablespoon chopped fresh flat-leaf parsley
1½ ounces Parmesan or Pecorino cheese, grated
Salt and freshly ground black pepper

TOMATO SAUCE
½ onion, finely diced
1 tablespoon vegetable oil
4 tomatoes, peeled, seeded, and diced
Dash of Worcestershire sauce
½ teaspoon dried Italian herbs
1 tablespoon Heinz Tomato Ketchup
Salt and freshly ground black pepper

Olive oil
Torn basil leaves, for garnish

To make the meatballs, put the turkey meat into a large bowl and add the onion, egg, bread crumbs, ketchup, parsley, and cheese. Season with salt and pepper, and then using your hands, mix all the ingredients together well. Form into balls in the palm of your hand, about the size of a golf ball—having wet hands prevents it all from sticking to you. Place the meatballs on waxed paper on a plate and chill in the fridge for up to 1 hour. You should get about 20 meatballs from this mixture.

In the meantime, to make the fresh tomato sauce, fry the onion in the vegetable oil until transparent. Add the tomatoes to the pan with the Worcestershire sauce, herbs, and ketchup, then taste and season with salt and plenty of pepper. Cook the sauce gently for about 5 minutes until you have a pulp that still retains a good texture. Put the sauce aside until you are ready to use it.

When ready to cook, preheat the oven to 350°F. Drizzle a baking sheet with a little olive oil and put the meatballs on the tray. Swirl them around to coat with the oil and bake for 40 minutes, or until golden. Divide the meatballs onto plates for your lucky guests, spoon over the warmed tomato sauce, and garnish with basil leaves.

The long and the short of it is...
no other ketchup tastes like Heinz

There's a new shape in Heinz Tomato Ketchup bottles–a 12-oz. bottle with a wider, easier-pouring neck. But whether you buy it in the new shape or the old shape it's still the same Heinz Tomato Ketchup. The ketchup that tastes different.

It tastes different because we make it different. We don't use artificial flavouring, preservatives,

artificial colouring, or thickeners. We use nothing but natural ingredients in Heinz Tomato Ketchup – ripe tomatoes (over a pound and a half in every 12-oz. bottle), homely spices, and Heinz know-how.

That's the difference.

And that's why, in any shape or form, no other ketchup tastes like Heinz.

MEAT

FIERY BARBECUE MARINADE

Hot summer days need this sizzling summer marinade for meat or vegetables.

MAKES 1 CUP

1 small onion, finely diced
2 Thai chiles, seeded and finely diced
1 tablespoon olive oil
4 tablespoons Heinz Tomato Ketchup
3/4 cup freshly squeezed orange juice
1 teaspoon orange marmalade
1 teaspoon soy sauce
1 tablespoon dark brown sugar
1 teaspoon dry mustard powder
1 tablespoon prepared horseradish
Pinch cayenne pepper

In a skillet, gently fry the onion and chiles in the olive oil for about 5 minutes. Add all the other ingredients, bring to a boil, then reduce the heat and let it bubble away for 3 to 4 minutes to slowly infuse all the flavors.

Refrigerate and use to marinate your barbecue meats and vegetables—it works especially well with pork, chicken, and butternut squash.

BEST BUDDIES #2

THE HOT DOG. The wienerwurst can be traced back to Vienna and the frankfurter to Frankfurt; the "dachshund" or "little dog" sausage has been attributed to a seventeenth-century Bavarian butcher. While mystery and lore shroud the true etymology of the sausage, what's certain is that by the twentieth century, its place as one of the most popular vendor foods was well and truly established, and no self-respecting stall owner would be without ketchup and mustard condiment bottles on the side.

SCHNITZEL WITH NOODLES

Pork tenderloin beaten wafer thin, nestled under a pile of tomato noodles.

SERVES 2

1 ($^3/_4$-pound) piece pork tenderloin
1 egg
1 cup white bread crumbs (stale ciabatta
  works really well)
$^2/_3$ pound dry egg noodles
2 teaspoons light soy sauce
3 tablespoons Heinz Tomato Ketchup
Vegetable oil, for frying
2 lemon wedges, for garnish

Cut the pork in half across the center to make two pieces. Using a sharp knife, cut down the length of each piece, making sure the knife only goes three-fourths of the way through the meat so that you can open it like a butterfly. Using a meat pounder, beat it out, teasing it from the center outward until it is no more than $^1/_4$ inch thick overall.

Prepare 2 shallow dishes large enough to hold the schnitzels. Break the egg into one dish and whisk. Spread the bread crumbs out in the other dish. Dunk each schnitzel first into the egg and then into the bread crumbs, making sure it is well coated with each. Place on waxed paper and chill in the fridge for 1 hour to set the coating. If you skip the chilling the coating will fall off when cooked.

When you are ready to cook, boil the noodles in salted water just until tender. Drain, add the soy sauce and ketchup, and mix well. Set aside and keep warm.

Heat 1 tablespoon of oil in a large frying pan over medium to high heat and add 1 schnitzel. Cook for 3 to 4 minutes on each side until the coating is golden and crispy. Keep warm while you cook the second schnitzel, adding a little more oil, if required.

Lay the schnitzels on warmed plates and place the noodles half on, half off one side of the schnitzel and garnish with a lemon wedge. This dish originates in Vienna, where the meat is served very thin and very big. *Guten appetit!*

1880–1905   1889–1894   1887–1895   1889–1910   1906–1910

GREEK LAMB TURNOVERS WITH FRESH OREGANO

Diced lamb, onion, garlic, and oregano encased in shimmering filo pastry.

SERVES 4 TO 6

1 medium onion, diced
Olive oil
1/2 pound potatoes, diced quite small
1 clove garlic, minced
1/2 pound lamb, trimmed of excess fat
    and cut into 1/2-inch cubes
1 plum tomato, peeled and diced
2 tablespoons Heinz Tomato Ketchup
Freshly ground black pepper
3/4 pound filo dough
1/4 cup (1/2 stick) butter, melted, for brushing
2 ounces feta cheese, cut into small cubes
Handful of fresh oregano

Preheat the oven to 350°F. Fry the onion in a little oil, add the potatoes and garlic, and continue cooking for 2 to 3 minutes, until the potatoes are just golden. Add the lamb, tomato, and ketchup and stir-fry for 10 minutes. Season with black pepper. Turn up the heat for a few minutes until the liquid has evaporated and you have a dryish mixture to fill the turnovers.

When using filo it is important not to let it dry out, so while you are working with the sheets keep the remainder under a clean, damp kitchen towel. Take 2 sheets, brush with melted butter, and lay a third sheet on the top. Now cut into 6-inch squares, putting 1 tablespoon of the lamb mixture (approximately 3 ounces), a cube of feta, and a few leaves of oregano into the center of each. Pick up one corner of the filo square and fold it in across the center. Then fold in the opposite corner and brush with butter to make it seal. Fold in the remaining 2 corners, pinching at the fold, and butter again to completely seal the turnover. Flip it over and place on the baking sheet so that the seams are underneath. Repeat until all the meat mixture is used up and brush the top of each turnover with melted butter.

Cover the baking sheet with foil and put in the oven. Bake for 1 hour, removing the foil for the last 10 minutes to make the pastry golden brown. Allow to cool a little before serving with a Greek salad or with minty yogurt on the side to make a great starter.

RIB-EYE STEAKS WITH STILTON SAUCE

Juicy steaks, perfectly seared with a blue cheese and tomato ketchup sauce.

SERVES 2

1 tablespoon butter
$1/4$ pound cultivated white mushrooms, sliced
$1/4$ pound Stilton cheese
2 tablespoons Heinz Tomato Ketchup
1 teaspoon runny honey
Freshly ground black pepper
1 tablespoon snipped fresh chives
Vegetable oil
2 rib-eye steaks, about $3/4$ inch thick

Melt the butter in a frying pan over medium heat. When it begins to froth, slide in the mushrooms and sauté for 3 to 4 minutes, until soft. Remove from the heat and tip the mushrooms with their buttery juices into a blender. Now crumble the Stilton into the blender along with the ketchup, honey, and a generous pinch of pepper. Blend until you have a smooth paste. To finish the sauce, stir in two-thirds of the chives.

Coat a griddle or heavy frying pan with a very small amount of vegetable oil and heat until just beginning to smoke. Slap in the steaks and cook for 4 to 5 minutes on each side for medium rare—adjust the cooking time if you want the steaks rare or well done.

Once the steaks are cooked, heat the broiler. Now spread the rich creamy mushroom and cheese sauce thickly over the steaks and pop under the broiler until the sauce just begins to bubble into brown specks—this won't take long. It is well worth resting the steaks for a couple of minutes before garnishing with the remaining chives and serving with homemade French fries.

HEINZ SELLS 650 MILLION BOTTLES OF KETCHUP EACH YEAR!

BANGERS AND MASH WITH RED ONION GRAVY

Perfect comfort food but with added zingy red onion gravy.

SERVES 2

1 medium red onion
Olive oil
1 teaspoon fresh thyme leaves
Salt and freshly ground black pepper
1 pound russet potatoes
$2/3$ pound good-quality sausages
$1 1/4$ cups good beef broth
$1/3$ cup red wine (if the cook can spare it!)
1 tablespoon Heinz Tomato Ketchup
2 tablespoons butter
1 rounded teaspoon Dijon mustard
2-3 tablespoons milk

Preheat the oven to 400°F. Cut the onion in half and then each half into four segments. Put them into a small roasting dish, drizzle with the oil, sprinkle the thyme over, and season with salt and pepper. Roast for 20 minutes.

Peel the potatoes and cut into chunks. Boil in lightly salted water for 15 to 20 minutes, until cooked through. Broil the sausages, turning as needed, for 15 to 20 minutes.

In the meantime, make the onion gravy. Bring the broth to a boil in a pan and add the red wine and ketchup. Decrease the heat a little and reduce the liquid by half to thicken it, about 10 minutes. Take the roasted onions out of the oven and add them to the gravy halfway through the cooking time, pressing them down with a fork to release the segments.

Drain the cooked potatoes, add the butter and mustard, and season with pepper. Add the milk gradually, until you have a smooth mixture, and mash well. At this stage you can use your ricer to make perfect creamy mashed potatoes or use a fairly open-mesh sieve and press the potato through with a wooden spoon to gain the same effect. (If you don't like mustard, try adding horseradish or chopped watercress.)

To serve this great traditional British dish, place a good dollop of mash on the plate, push the sausages into the mash at jaunty angles, and pour over the rich onion gravy.

ITALIAN SAUSAGE AND WHITE BEAN CASSEROLE

Great sausages, big juicy beans, slow-cooked in a delicious, rich tomato sauce.

SERVES 4

2 tablespoons olive oil
1 pound Italian pork sausages
1 clove garlic, finely chopped
2 shallots, finely sliced
1 medium carrot, diced
1 stalk celery, diced
$1/2$ teaspoon smoked paprika
1 ($14^1/2$-ounce) can chopped Italian tomatoes
2 tablespoons maple syrup
3 tablespoons Heinz Tomato Ketchup
$1^3/4$ cups vegetable broth
1 heaping teaspoon dried Italian herbs
1 ($14^1/2$-ounce) can cannellini beans, drained
Salt
1 teaspoon Dijon mustard
4 slices sourdough toast, for serving

Preheat the oven to 300°F.

Heat the oil in a deep frying pan and gently cook the sausages until just golden. Transfer to an ovenproof casserole dish. Add the garlic, shallots, carrot, and celery to the remaining oil in the pan and sauté them gently for 5 minutes. Add the paprika, tomatoes, maple syrup, ketchup, broth, and herbs to the vegetables, mix them all together, and tip the mixture into the casserole dish.

Finally, add the beans to the casserole together with a pinch of salt and the mustard. Stir everything gently; put the lid on the casserole and cook in the oven for 1 hour; you should have a great deep red sauce around the sausages and beans. Remove from the oven and let stand for 5 minutes.

When you're ready to serve, toast 4 thick slices of sourdough bread and spoon the delicious sausages, beans, and their sauce over the toast for each serving.

LET'S HEAR IT FOR BANGERS.

A PAT ON THE BACK FOR THE HOT DOG.

GOULASH WITH HORSERADISH AND HERB DUMPLINGS

Strips of beef in a rich tomato sauce with fluffy dumplings.

SERVES 6

GOULASH
2 pounds beef chuck, cut into 1$\frac{1}{2}$-inch cubes
2 tablespoons all-purpose flour
Salt and freshly ground black pepper
2 tablespoons butter
1 tablespoon vegetable oil
2 large onions, chopped
1 red bell pepper, sliced
2 tablespoons Heinz Tomato Ketchup
1 tablespoon paprika
2$\frac{1}{2}$ cups good beef broth

DUMPLINGS
$\frac{1}{2}$ cup self-rising flour
Generous pinch salt
$\frac{1}{4}$ cup ($\frac{1}{2}$ stick) butter
2 rounded teaspoons prepared horseradish
$\frac{1}{2}$ teaspoon chopped fresh parsley
$\frac{1}{2}$ teaspoon chopped fresh oregano
$\frac{1}{2}$ teaspoon chopped fresh thyme
$\frac{1}{2}$ teaspoon chopped fresh chives
(If you don't have the fresh herbs you can use
   1 heaping teaspoon of dried Italian herbs.)
4 to 5 tablespoons water

$\frac{2}{3}$ cup sour cream
Handful of fresh chives, snipped

To make the goulash, preheat the oven to 300°F. Put the beef into a large bowl and sift the flour over it. Add salt and pepper and toss to coat each piece of meat. Heat the butter and oil in a large heavy frying pan and brown the beef in batches, separating the chunks of meat as they cook. Using a slotted spoon, transfer the meat to a casserole dish (or Dutch oven) wide enough to accommodate the dumplings later.

Add the onions to the same pan and fry for 5 to 6 minutes, until soft. Add the bell pepper and cook for a few minutes more, then transfer to the casserole. Back to the pan, add the ketchup, paprika, and broth and bring it all to a boil, scraping the bottom to deglaze the pan, gathering up the good flavored bits. Pour the mixture over the beef in the casserole, stir, cover, and cook in the oven for 1$\frac{1}{2}$ hours, until the beef is tender.

While the beef is cooking, you can prepare the dumplings. Sift the flour and salt into a bowl and add the butter, horseradish, and herbs and mix well. Add enough of the water to make a firm but pliable dough. Using floured hands, form into 8 golf ball–size dumplings.

Remove the casserole from the oven and increase the temperature to 350°F. Drop the dumplings into the casserole, where they will settle on top of the goulash. Replace the lid and return to the oven for 15 minutes, until the dumplings are puffy and fluffy.

Lift out the dumplings with a slotted spoon and put them on warm serving plates. Stir the sour cream into the goulash, spoon onto plates, and garnish with the chopped chives.

TOMATO-CRUSTED RACK OF LAMB WITH BABY VEGETABLES

A perfect Sunday dinner with loads of garden flavors.

SERVES 2

1 (6-bone) rack of lamb
2 tablespoons Heinz Tomato Ketchup
1 tablespoon chopped fresh mint
1 tablespoon chopped fresh flat-leaf parsley
1 green onion, finely chopped
8 baby new potatoes
8 baby zucchini
8 baby carrots
10 green olives, pitted and halved
Zest of 1/2 lemon
Olive oil
Sea salt and freshly ground black pepper

This recipe uses baby zucchini and baby carrots, but any baby vegetables in season would be good.

Preheat the oven to 400°F. Pat the fat side of the lamb with paper towels to thoroughly dry. Score the lamb in both directions, making diamond shapes in the fat (much like you would to make ham). Spread it with ketchup and push into the slits with a knife. Mix together the mint, parsley, and green onion and press the mixture over the ketchup. Place the lamb herb side up in a roasting pan and roast for 10 minutes.

Remove the pan from the oven and add the potatoes, zucchini, and carrots, top with the olives and lemon zest, drizzle with olive oil, and season with salt and pepper. Return the pan to the oven and roast the vegetables with the lamb for 25 minutes longer. This will cook the lamb to pink, so add 5 to 15 minutes if you like it more well done.

Remove the pan from the oven and allow the lamb to rest for 5 minutes, keeping the vegetables warm. Arrange the vegetables neatly on warm serving plates. Slice the lamb into chops, and arrange next to the vegetables.

KETCHUP CAN BE FOUND IN THE KITCHENS OF 97% OF AMERICAN HOMES!

There's more to Heinz than meets the eye

Over 2 lb. of pampered, perfect tomatoes go into every 15-oz. bottle of Heinz Tomato Ketchup.

Tomatoes highlighted with a hint of spice and vinegar and subtly improved with a touch of seasoning.

But there's another touch which is even more important. The Heinz touch.

It's a matter of balance and blending, of care and cooking. Combined with the finest ingredients it makes the ketchup with the best-loved flavour in the world.

You can't see the Heinz touch. But you can taste it. Ask your family.

No other ketchup has the Heinz touch

BALSAMIC BARBECUE RIBS

**Classic pork spareribs with a sweet
sensation in the marinade.**

SERVES 4 TO 6

4 pounds pork spareribs

SAUCE
1 onion, finely diced
Olive oil
1 (14$\frac{1}{2}$-ounce) can diced tomatoes
6 tablespoons dark brown sugar
$\frac{1}{3}$ cup balsamic vinegar
Juice of $\frac{1}{2}$ lime
4 tablespoons Heinz Tomato Ketchup
1 teaspoon chile powder
2 tablespoons dark rum or bourbon

Preheat the oven to 400°F. Lay the ribs in a
single layer on a rack over a large roasting pan
and roast for 30 minutes. It is important to use
a rack to allow the fat to drain.

While the ribs are roasting, you can make
the sauce. Sweat the onion with a drizzle of
olive oil in a saucepan until just translucent,
but not browned. Now add all the other sauce
ingredients to the pan, increase the heat, and
when it starts to bubble decrease the heat
and simmer for 10 minutes.

Remove the ribs from the oven and carefully
drain off the fat. Tip the ribs from the rack back
into the roasting pan and pour the sauce over
them, making sure they are well coated.

Decrease the oven temperature to 350°F
and cook the ribs for 1 to 1$\frac{1}{4}$ hours longer, until
tender, turning in the sauce from time to time.

If you are planning a barbecue, you can
cook these in advance and give them a last
sizzle over the hot coals.

SWEET AND SOUR PORK

A real Chinese favorite with a fabulous homemade sweet and sour sauce.

SERVES 2 TO 3

2 tablespoons sesame oil
1 pound pork loin, cut into 1-inch cubes
1 green onion, finely chopped
2 teaspoons finely chopped fresh ginger
1 clove garlic, minced
1 tablespoon light soy sauce
2 tablespoons sugar
3 tablespoons white wine vinegar
2 tablespoons Heinz Tomato Ketchup
1/4 cup water
Noodles or rice, for serving
Pineapple, broiled, for serving

Heat the oil in a wok, then fry the pork until any traces of fat are just golden and crispy, about 4 to 5 minutes, ensuring that the meat is cooked through. Remove from the wok with a slotted spoon and drain on paper towels.

Pour out any excess oil, leaving a coating in the wok, and add the green onion, ginger, and garlic and stir-fry for a couple of minutes. Add the soy sauce, sugar, vinegar, ketchup, and water and bring to a boil. Decrease the heat and allow the sauce to reduce and thicken slightly.

Return the pork to the wok and stir it in the hot sauce for 2 minutes. Serve over noodles or rice with chunks of broiled pineapple.

A TIGHT SQUEEZE!

Heinz packs more than a staggering pound of ripe, fresh tomatoes into every fourteen-ounce glass bottle of tomato ketchup that it makes. That's a tight fit! And to keep ketchup lovers happy with enough of their favorite red condiment, Heinz uses a quantity of fresh tomatoes sufficient to fill an Olympic-size swimming pool—every day of the year. It guarantees a great taste, but it also means it's a potent source of the powerful antioxidant lycopene.

No one grows Ketchup like Heinz.

No one
grows
Ketchup
like

VEGETARIAN

Now Mrs. Beeton gets together with Heinz to cook with ketchup

It's the new, exciting way to add that touch of variety to your meals. Rich, red Heinz Tomato Ketchup in the cooking makes a delicious change in your favourite dishes!

We've taken some of the famous recipes from the 1961 Mrs. Beeton's Cookery Book. But we've added Heinz Tomato Ketchup. And presto! The same delicious meal—but with a difference.

Here, for a fascinating change, is Mrs. Beeton's Chicken in Casserole . . . with Heinz Tomato Ketchup. It's an easy treat to give your family, so why not make it tonight?

A REFRIGERATOR A DAY TO BE WON DURING SEPTEMBER in the new "Cook with Ketchup" competition! And there are more delicious recipes, too. Entry forms from your local Heinz stockist.

HEINZ 57 Tomato Ketchup

CHICKEN IN CASSEROLE

1 chicken	1 shallot
1 oz. flour	2 oz. chopped mushrooms
Salt and pepper	1 pint stock
2 oz. butter or dripping	2 tablespoons
4-6 oz. streaky bacon	Heinz Tomato Ketchup

Joint the chicken, dip joints in flour and seasoning. Melt the fat in a casserole; fry the bacon, cut in strips; add chicken, mushrooms and chopped shallot. Fry until golden brown, turning when necessary. Add hot stock, sufficient just to cover the chicken, simmer until tender . . . about 1½ hours. Add 2 tablespoons of Heinz Tomato Ketchup, bring to the boil, and correct the seasoning.

Serve in the casserole. 6 helpings.

GOLDEN EGG BOAT CURRY

A rich creamy curry floating with spicy golden eggs.

SERVES 4

2 tablespoons vegetable oil
2 medium onions, roughly chopped
2 cloves garlic, minced
3 tablespoons Madras curry powder
4 tablespoons Heinz Tomato Ketchup
1 tablespoon brown sugar
1 ($14^1/2$-ounce) can chopped tomatoes
$3/4$ cup water
Salt and freshly ground black pepper
4 tablespoons Greek yogurt
$1/3$ pound frozen peas
8 eggs, hard boiled, shelled, and halved
Garam masala, for sprinkling
Handful of fresh cilantro, roughly chopped

Heat the oil in a pan and fry the onions and garlic for about 10 minutes, or until soft and just browning. Remove from the heat and allow to cool a little, then grind in a food processor for 30 seconds to make a puree.

Return the puree to the pan, add the curry powder and ketchup, and sizzle for a couple of minutes. (It seems quite apt to add ketchup to an Asian dish, as the word originates from the Chinese word for sauce.) Add the sugar, tomatoes, and water and bring to a boil. Decrease the heat and simmer, covered, for 15 minutes, until you have a rich sauce. Check the seasoning and add salt and pepper to taste.

Stir the yogurt and peas into the curry sauce and simmer for a few minutes longer. Add the eggs to the pan, spoon the sauce over them to coat, and keep simmering for 3 to 4 minutes longer.

Serve the curry sprinkled with a little garam masala and scattered with cilantro. This is great served with saffron rice and mango chutney.

CAULIFLOWER FRITTERS WITH SWEET CHILE DIP

Delicate florets dipped in cumin batter and served with a perfectly sweet dip.

SERVES 4

DIP
4 tablespoons Greek yogurt
1 teaspoon mint sauce
1 tablespoon Heinz Tomato Ketchup
$1/2$ teaspoon lemon juice
$1/2$ red chile, seeded and very finely diced
Pinch sugar
Salt and freshly ground black pepper

FRITTERS
$3/4$ pound fresh cauliflower, broken
   into bite-size florets
$1/2$ cup gram flour (chickpea flour)
$1/4$ cup rice flour
$1/4$ teaspoon baking powder
Pinch cumin seeds
$1/2$ teaspoon curry powder
$3/4$ cup water
Vegetable oil, for deep-frying

To make the dip, combine all the ingredients in a suitable dish, cover, and chill in the fridge.

To make the fritters, bring a pan of salted water to a boil and lower the cauliflower florets in. Boil for 2 minutes, drain, and cool on paper towels.

Sift the gram flour, rice flour, and baking powder into a bowl, then add the cumin seeds and curry powder. Gradually add enough of the water to make a smooth batter. Set aside the batter for 20 minutes.

Heat the vegetable oil to 375°F, ideally in a deep-fat fryer. Using a fork, spear each floret and dip it in the batter, rolling it around to get it completely coated. Allow any excess batter to drop off and then, using a knife, slide the floret off the fork and into the hot oil. Fry in batches for 6 to 8 minutes, until golden brown, moving them around once or twice in the oil with a slotted spoon. Remove and drain on paper towels.

Serve the florets warm and the dip chilled for a perfect starter or great accompaniment to curry dishes.

BLOODY MARY MACARONI

Thick tubes of pasta married to a spicy vodka, tomato, and celery sauce.

SERVES 4

SAUCE
1 medium onion, diced
Olive oil
1 (14^1/$_2$-ounce) can chopped
   Italian plum tomatoes
^{1}/$_3$ cup vodka
1 tablespoon sherry
2 tablespoons Heinz Tomato Ketchup
^{1}/$_4$ teaspoon Worcestershire sauce
Dash of Tabasco Sauce
^{1}/$_2$ teaspoon celery salt
Freshly ground black pepper
1 teaspoon dried Italian herbs

1 vegetable bouillon cube
^{3}/$_4$ pound macaroni
Freshly ground black pepper
Handful of torn basil leaves, for garnish
Parmesan shavings, for garnish

To make the sauce, in a large frying pan, cook the onion in a little oil, then add the rest of the sauce ingredients except the herbs. Increase the heat and cook fairly rapidly for 8 to 10 minutes, until you can no longer smell alcohol in the steam and the sauce has thickened. Stir in the herbs, remove the pan from the heat, and set aside.

Bring a pan of water to a boil, crumble in the bouillon cube, and add the macaroni. Cook for 8 to 10 minutes, until the pasta is just al dente. Drain and drizzle with a little olive oil and season with pepper.

Reheat the sauce if necessary, serve the macaroni in warmed bowls, and pour over the sauce. Garnish with the basil leaves and Parmesan shavings.

A WELL-TRAVELLED SAUCE

The word *ketchup* possibly has its origins in the Chinese word *ke-tsiap*, a pickled fish sauce, the savory taste of which was the mingled flavors of spicy brine and fish. It traveled from China to Malaysia, where it became *kechap*. It ventured onward to Indonesia, where it was *ketjap*. In the seventeenth century, Dutch and English sailors so enjoyed slathering their foods with it that they took it aboard with them, back to the

SPINACH, PEPPER, AND MUSHROOM TERRINE

Layers of vibrant vegetable colors: rosy red and leafy green.

SERVES 6 TO 8

2 pounds red bell peppers
2 tablespoons Heinz Tomato Ketchup
$1/2$ cup stale bread crumbs
4 egg whites
1 pound cremini mushrooms, sliced
Olive oil
1 teaspoon chopped fresh basil
1 teaspoon chopped fresh oregano
   (or generous pinch of dried)
Sea salt and freshly ground black pepper
$3/4$ pound fresh spinach leaves, stemmed

To peel the peppers, place them under a hot broiler and scorch them all over. Transfer them to a paper bag and seal it up. After a few minutes you will be able to remove the skins quite easily with a small knife. Put the peppers in a blender together with the ketchup, half the bread crumbs, and half the egg whites and blend thoroughly. Transfer the mixture to a bowl and keep cool.

Cook the mushrooms gently in a frying pan with a little olive oil for 5 minutes, then increase the heat, stirring often, and cook for 10 minutes more, or until all the moisture has evaporated. Allow to cool a little and then in a clean blender jar, blend the mushrooms together with the remaining bread crumbs and remaining egg whites until you have a good smooth mixture. Add the herbs, season with salt and pepper, and blend very briefly. Set aside and keep cool.

Preheat the oven to 400°F. Blanch the spinach for 1 minute in a large pan of salted boiling water, then drain and press out as much moisture as possible on paper towels. Line a 1-pound terrine with parchment and spoon in half the pepper puree. Lay half of the spinach all over, then add all the mushroom mixture, followed by the rest of the spinach and finally the remaining pepper mixture. Cover with parchment and bake in the oven for 1 hour.

Leave to cool in the terrine for a few hours, and then turn out onto a serving plate.

West. They unveiled their booty once home, and the sauce drew comparisons with soy sauce and with Worcestershire sauce. The sauce was modified over the years. British alternatives included the brine of pickled mushrooms, anchovies, oysters, and walnuts—these were often quite sharp to the taste buds. Sometime around the 1700s came the addition of tomatoes, and ketchup as we know it today was born. The terms *catchup*, *catsup*, and *ketchup* all relate back to the original foreign borrowing of *ke-tsiap*, and all remain in use today.

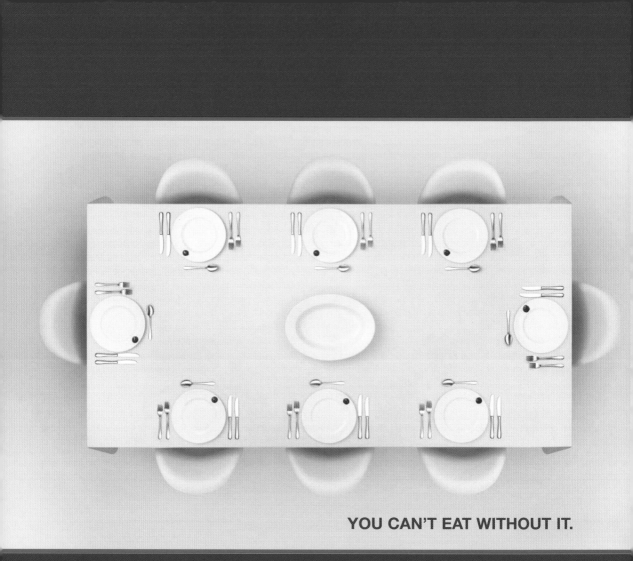

YOU CAN'T EAT WITHOUT IT.

VEGGIE MOUSSAKA

A confection of Mediterranean vegetables packed with sunshine flavors.

SERVES 4

1 tablespoon olive oil
1 red onion, chopped
1 clove garlic (optional), chopped
1 leek, cut into 1/2-inch slices
1 red bell pepper, cut into 1-inch pieces
1 green bell pepper, cut into 1-inch pieces
1/3 pound mushrooms, roughly chopped
1 (14 1/2-ounce) can chopped tomatoes
2 tablespoons Heinz Tomato Ketchup
1 (14 1/2-ounce) can cannellini beans, drained
1 teaspoon chopped fresh thyme
1 teaspoon chopped fresh oregano
Salt and freshly ground black pepper
1 large (or 2 small) eggplants, sliced
1 cup Greek yogurt
2 ounces feta cheese, crumbled
1 large egg

Preheat the oven to 350°F. Heat half the oil in a pan and sauté the onion until soft. Add the garlic and leek and cook for 3 to 4 minutes, then add the peppers, mushrooms, tomatoes, and ketchup. Cook gently for 10 minutes, then add the beans and herbs. Season with salt and pepper.

Heat the broiler and, using the remaining oil, brush both sides of the eggplant slices, then pop them under the broiler for a few minutes on each side, or until golden. (Eggplants absorb a huge amount of oil if fried, so it is much better to broil or bake them.)

Lay half the eggplant slices on the bottom of a large shallow ovenproof dish, then cover with half of the vegetable mixture. Repeat with the rest of the eggplant and top with the remaining vegetable mixture.

Whisk together the yogurt, half the feta cheese, and the egg. Pour this over the veggie mixture and spread to cover with the back of a spoon. Sprinkle the rest of the feta cheese over the top and season with pepper. Bake for 40 to 50 minutes, until the top is golden brown. Allow to cool slightly before serving with a crunchy romaine lettuce and watercress salad.

BAKERY

HERBY SCONES WITH TOMATO AND FETA

Savory scones for lunchtime soups.

MAKES 10 SCONES

$1/2$ cup whole wheat flour
$7/8$ cup self-rising flour
1 teaspoon baking powder
$1/2$ teaspoon mustard powder
Pinch paprika
2 tablespoons olive oil
$1/3$ pound feta cheese, cut into
   small cubes
1 teaspoon chopped fresh thyme
1 teaspoon chopped fresh parsley
Handful of black olives (about 8),
   pitted and chopped
3 tablespoons Heinz Tomato Ketchup
1 egg
$1/3$ cup milk

Preheat the oven to 425°F. You will need a 2 to 2$1/2$-inch cookie cutter and a lightly oiled baking sheet.

Sift the flours and baking powder into a large bowl, then add the mustard and paprika. Gradually add the oil and mix until you have a lumpy crumb mixture. Next, add two-thirds of the feta cheese, the fresh herbs, and the olives.

In a small bowl beat together the ketchup, egg, and milk and add this gradually to the flour mixture, leaving a teaspoon or so for brushing later. Using your hands or a wooden spoon, blend together to form a dough that is soft but not too sticky.

Flour a board and roll out the dough until it is about 1 inch thick. Cut out 10 rounds, rerolling and using up the odd bits. Lay the rounds on the baking sheet and brush each with the reserved egg and milk mixture. Crumble the remaining feta cheese on top of them and put on the top rack of the oven to bake for 12 to 15 minutes, until golden. Cool a little on a wire rack before munching.

PULP-TASTIC KETCHUP

Quentin Tarantino obviously has a penchant for ketchup—he managed to squeeze two references to the glorious red stuff into his film *Pulp Fiction*. First, an exchange between his two hitmen characters, exploring the differences between American and Dutch consumer cultures: Vincent: *"You know what they put on French fries in Holland instead of ketchup?"* Jules: *"What?"* Vincent: *"Mayonnaise."* Jules: *"Goddamn."* Vincent: *"I've seen 'em do it, man. And I don't mean a little bit on the side of the plate . . ."*

PARMESAN STRAWS

Cheesy twists of flaky pastry—perfect dippers.

MAKES ABOUT 20 CHEESE STRAWS

$1/3$ pound grated Parmesan cheese
1 pound chilled puff pastry
4 tablespoons Heinz Tomato Ketchup

Preheat the oven to 425°F. Dust your work surface with half the Parmesan, place the pastry on top, and cut in half. Roll out the halves until the pastry is about $1/2$ inch thick, then spread all over with the ketchup. Sprinkle with the remaining Parmesan and fold the pastry sheets over to sandwich the ketchup and roll out again to about $1/2$ inch thick.

Lay some parchment on 2 large baking sheets. Cut the pastry widthwise into $1/2$-inch strips and, taking each strip by the ends, rotate into a tight rope twist and lay on the baking sheets, pressing the ends down onto the sheet to secure them. Continue until you have used all the pastry. Chill in the fridge for 20 minutes, and then put straight into the hot oven. Bake for 10 to 15 minutes, until golden all over. Cool a little on a rack and then serve while still warm.

Then, there's a joke and a promise that it won't be funny:
"Three tomatoes are walking down the street—a poppa tomato, a momma tomato, and a little baby tomato. Baby tomato starts lagging behind. Poppa tomato gets angry, goes over to the baby tomato, and squishes him . . . and says, 'Ketchup.'"
Most, of course, would claim that Tarantino's real love of ketchup is all too evident in his films: it's usually spattered by the gallon across his characters as each meets his gruesome end!

TEARING SHARING FOCACCIA

**Ham and cheese bread marbled with
tomato ketchup.**

MAKES 1 ROUND

2 teaspoons dried yeast
1¼ cups water
2½ cups bread flour
1½ teaspoons salt
3 tablespoons olive oil, plus
    additional as needed
2 tablespoons Heinz Tomato Ketchup
2 ounces cheddar cheese, crumbled
2 ounces smoked ham, roughly diced
8 small rosemary top sprigs
Pinch coarse salt

In a small bowl sprinkle the yeast into two-thirds of the water. Leave for 5 minutes, then stir to dissolve. Sift the flour and salt into a large bowl, make a well in the center, and pour in the yeast mixture and 3 tablespoons of olive oil. Mix the flour by working from the outside into the center and add the remaining water to make a sticky dough. Turn out onto a lightly floured surface and knead for about 10 minutes, or until the dough is smooth and elastic. Put into a lightly oiled bowl, cover with a kitchen towel, and leave at room temperature until the dough has doubled in size, up to 2 hours.

Punch down or deflate the dough by pressing down in the center with your knuckles. Divide it into 2 rounds and make a circle of the dough between your hands, tucking it in and under as you go; you need to do this for about 5 minutes. Set aside to rest for 10 minutes.

Gently roll out each half to create roughly 8-inch rounds. Put 1 round on a lightly oiled baking sheet and spread with most of the ketchup, then scatter with the cheese and ham, adding several dollops of the remaining ketchup for the final flourish. Seal the sandwich of dough with the other round and pinch together around the edges. Cover loosely with a kitchen towel and leave to rise for about 30 minutes, until doubled in size.

Preheat the oven to 400°F.

Press gently into the surface of the dough with your fingertips to make little dimples, pop in the mini sprigs of rosemary, then scatter with coarse salt and drizzle with a little more olive oil. Bake for 30 to 40 minutes, until golden. Remove from the oven, drizzle right away with a little more olive oil, and serve warm to tear and share.

INDEX

10

Ten Speed Press
PO Box 7123
Berkeley, California 94707
www.tenspeed.com

First published in Great Britain in 2007 by
Absolute Press, Scarborough House,
29 James Street West, Bath BA1 2BT, England

Distributed in Canada by Ten Speed Press
Canada.

Cover design by Chloe Rawlins
Text design by Matt Inwood
Food styling by Claire Ptak
Prop styling by Cynthia Inions

Library of Congress Cataloging-in-Publication
Data
Hartley, Paul, 1947-
  The Heinz tomato ketchup cookbook /
Paul Hartley.
      p. cm.
  "A collection of 40 recipes using Heinz Tomato
Ketchup, along with Heinz history and trivia"—
Provided by publisher.
  Includes index.
  Originally published: Bath, England : Absolute
Press, 2007.
  ISBN 978-1-58008-936-4
  1. Cookery (Ketchup) 2. H.J. Heinz Company.
I. Title.
  TX819.K48H37 2008
  641.8'14—dc22
                                              2008012925

Printed in China
First printing, 2008

1 2 3 4 5 6 7 8 9 10 — 12 11 10 09 08